HERE ON EARTH

WESLEYAN NEW POETS

HERE ON EARTH

KAREN BRENNAN

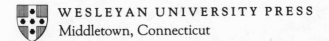

WESLEYAN UNIVERSITY PRESS
Middletown, Connecticut

Special thanks to Cynthia Hogue, Julie Willson,
Steve Orlen and John Palumbo for their help and
encouragement.

Some of these poems previously appeared in *Black Warrior Review;*
Clarion; Columbia, A Magazine of Poetry & Prose; Iowa Woman;
Ploughshares; Seneca Review; Sequoia Review; Sonora Review; Tucson
Guide Quarterly; Woman Poet: The West II.

This book is supported by a grant from the National Endowment for the Arts.

LIBRARY OF CONGRESS CATALOGING-IN-PUBLICATION DATA

Brennan, Karen, 1941–
    Here on earth / Karen Brennan.—1st ed.
        p. cm.
    ISBN 0-8195-2155-8 ISBN 0-8195-1156-0 (pbk.)
    I. Title.
PS3552.R378H4 1988   87-36443
811'.54—DC19   CIP

All inquiries and permissions requests should be addressed to
the Publisher, Wesleyan University Press, 110 Mt. Vernon Street,
Middletown, Connecticut 06457

Manufactured in the United States of America

FIRST EDITION

WESLEYAN NEW POETS

For my sons, Chris and Geoff

Contents

Is it not possible—I often wonder—that things we have felt with great intensity have an existence independent of our minds; are in fact still in existence?

—VIRGINIA WOOLF, *Moments of Being*

HERE ON EARTH

A Beautiful Way of Looking
at Something Starts

A beautiful way of looking at something starts at the throat. Always, the tenderest part first like when you try to fathom what the sky's doing precisely and you begin with a cloud. That simple. In it and not of it, exactly. Forming a context like the mathematical perfection of walls in the living room, an angular certain fireplace, the blaze like triangle after shifting triangle. And you are in the center, reading or sipping something, whoever you are.

ONE

History Lesson

Before the real world was invented
tourists invented a fake one.
They began at the center
which poses for its solution
a sphere, and worked outwards,
carving in fountains and monuments,
a few palms less ordinary than
real ones, and a sky that was colorless,
not having suffered enough.
It was haphazard,
this way of doing—
a hayloft, then snacks;
a woman streamed
from an umbrella and the rain
went up so high you could not
think of it without abstraction.
Nevertheless, kindness in this world
prevailed, and restaurants came
almost alive. A bird flew, a tree delivered
nearly enough curiosity, the river
once a hollow shape in someone's palm
bravely chose a direction. There was practically
nothing unheard of—a rustle beneath a bush or
the strange, unearthly crackle of a moth
whose clever wise face glittered
on the screen; and inside the quiet
lamplight, the tablecloth, the paperback
dictionary.

Rocketing Back and Forth the Rabbits

Rocketing back and forth the rabbits
are tired and yearning for transformation.
Nevertheless, they pop up in each major city
before the handkerchiefs and the fixed
deck and in two zips a woman is halved
like an onion and a blue-suited man
takes an elevator to Antwerp, gets
his quarters back in diamonds.

That's who we are when the lights go out,
divided women or impossible travelers
partly outside ourselves and part
ordinary, settled on some aisle or other
letting the play unravel or dissolve
us—which in real life is always
about to occur—

And this is what we love,
the sheer terrible irony of every performance
and how we can alter things
by just clapping along or squinting
or taking a walk like we did as kids
near the flat rocks of a park
watching sailboats slip from the notion
of diminishing angles
                              in back of which
the horizon simply *was*—
no longing there, but a wealth of enigma
defying even the bravest among us.

Chaucer's Black Knight Is Still Weeping in the 14th Century

And this is what he said: he said
I have of sorwe so greet woon
that joy gete I nevere noon.
He said it in the woods. His head

was hooded blankly in a hood
to decorate the lines of grief
romantically. His disbelief
was like a dime—believing could

he not believe? He'd never been
so clearheaded, so terrified—
so under chinks of sky, and skyed
(without imagination) in,

became reflective; even snakes
were creeping up attentively
and *douves* and *whelpes* loved to see
how still he sat, his eyes like lakes.

Rain, Bach, the Desert and the City

It rains in the desert this morning
and I am thinking *cities*, a dog
squatting by the garbage or those apartment views
of walls, occasionally a window carved
into the sides, occasionally an open curtain where
you see a man move by deliberately,
pick up a towel, dry his hair. In the privacy
of your vision, he has lost his—and so, as now,
the world is reflected through our interruption
of it. Now, the rain falling in thin weary
lines and on the bricks little puddles and
I'm listening to a Bach violin concerto, all
the sweeping gestures of joy, not
joy exactly, not exactly joy—
so what do we do when words, like rain,
fail to retrieve us, when loping backwards
or gasping for air we find we have merely
to say something: exactly what we mean to say,
all the difficulties, the tightness around the chest
and wrists, the complication of fact and vision,
like here is the rain, like Bach's virtuoso
violinists, like the word joy which, in missing so
poignantly our feeling about it, is nonetheless musical,
almost perfect.   In the city, the man
traverses his apartment, empty except for a small
chest of drawers, a towel, a kitten near the bookshelves.
It's raining in the desert and we think naturally
of familiar and continuous solitude
where the sky has nothing to do with us—the man
sitting at the window and remembering more
imperfectly each time—

Tucson Oranges

They seem like shady simple souls
and half unhappy here, but it's only
oranges we overlooked, only the view
of what we wasted this winter. Meanwhile
everything else is exemplary—jasmine
spill into shadows on schedule, the old
bicycle is brighter than it was before
and the lawn is newer.
                        Nevertheless, nothing
exactly appears to prove a portion of our landscape
beautiful. We borrow a bravery from words,
unluckily believe that lifelessness belongs
to another order. But oranges, refusing
to fall or forgotten, are figures of longing—
permanent, private apparitions we cannot
hope to hold in our hearts for long.

The Order of Things

The bright colors of the flowers reproduce,
without violence, the pure form of the sky.

1

In the garden labor continues.
Tulips, miniature iris.
In front of bougainvillaea
she imagines anemones
clanking up the brick steps.
Spring and a few drifting clouds.
From the lawn chair plumes of smoke
jitter along
and is she dreaming
or is the sun really
spinning in a socket, the bee-shaped
platoon of airplanes shooting terrifyingly
through? The way nothing is quite paradise
on her earth—

2

She is pacing the brick patio,
counting the bricks, her mind dazed
in the face of so much texture.
And isn't this the season for looking
back, a time to overcome
things? Headaches with vinegar packs
or for luck a little bone meal
sprinkled 'round the bulb bed:
The bright colors of the flowers
reproduce, without violence,
the pure form of the sky
and the future reels toward the mind
who forms a vision

of exactly how it will appear
in batches of one-color blooms
arranged according to height and leaf length
which is why
come cold Autumn dirt freeze
we dig under.

3
After the fade and after
she scrapes old leaves away
there are only soft bulbs underneath,
which are eyeless
like the heart itself,
which find some solace
from the common notion of death and strength.
Leonardo da Vinci
puzzled about flowers, wondered
how the spirit moved lighter
than air, and about displacements
of certain weights, roots, earth, or
the simple avenue of a river flowing
downhill and if it suddenly, by means
of wind or otherwise, could shoot
another way.
Flowers grow always
upward, she can tell him —

Here on Earth

Here on earth where perfection is the story
of each failure, think of it as flowers, how
petals collapsing in the small angle of light
around the vase disappear eventually
and how in the wilderness of what remains
there are things which tenderly seek our voices.

Waiting for a Bus,
You Dream of the Future

It has to be easier
after a few years, we tell ourselves,
then when the shoreline
has crept up and hotels like
the Savoy Hilton have fallen over.
Meanwhile we are left with
all this atmosphere, dust, neon
blinking as frailly as moths do—
and creeping forward with what
trepidation can we identify
each other as brave or glamorous?
No. It's harder than you imagine
because up close
things blur and/or link up,
so what's the use?
                        Near the bus stop
a woman waves a kerchief
which the breeze enflames
and the bus comes like a
baritone. I sit here writing
it all down because you
never know how quickly
one time passes into another,
then mourns itself.
Nevertheless, too many loose ends
called from the weight of the world
are tiresome, even
ridiculous—
seeing as they are
a part of something and so,
not distinct, or even temporary—
Imagine, though, all
the great hotels falling in the ocean,
what then? Then what would happen?

The World, You Think,
Wants to Be More Graceful

The world, you think, wants to be more graceful.
It aches for gracefulness. You see it in
the continuous line of the mountain
and in the way the poplars want to shake free
and in the way the cars in the streets
want to exceed the speed limit and lift

off like DC-10s. Even as planes lift
off they want, perhaps, to explode, graceful
and natural as supernovas, above streets
we've constructed and cars that ride in
them. But you say we are completely free
tonight. Look at the moon, you say, the mountain

is what the moon achieves here. The mountain
is where we are headed, where we will lift
off the speed that holds us, endure a free
sense of ourselves, therefore, to feel graceful
not hopeful. When Wordsworth wrote he wrote in
order to recover himself and streets

for him were flukes of glory, not the streets
we construct. Still, Wordsworth whom the mountain
moved so absolutely went "singly in
his ministry across the ocean." Lift
up our voices? Recovery? Words are graceful
only because they come to us free,

essentially, of yearning to be free.
You don't believe me though. You are like streets
pretending to come alive, our graceful

illusion, you say. We drive toward the mountain
where stars are no closer: I want to lift
myself, miles miles, away from you. Though in

spite of ourselves and in lieu of these streets
we are free to avoid, groves of mountain
deer are waiting, lift their eyes, are graceful.

Lace Curtains

Once I put up one
I had to have twenty or at least
12. Every window streaming in lace
like a baby's christening, the lace
of visions where what you see
is open to interpretation; blurred
eucalyptus, for example, or the soft reliable
line of the mountains, fragmentary sky,
dreamy swish of automobiles reeling
through lace curtains. I had to have
12, one for each window so that
wherever I looked it would seem
less stationary, so I could imagine
that all this—the house, the windows,
the random beautiful objects like the
cup or the onion peel or the book—
was open to interpretation . . .
All this—the house, the windows,
the random beautiful objects like the
cup . . .

TWO

Nijinsky at the Windshield

He began in the corner of the room
    and worked sideways, along the glorious
tables, the wine glasses, the rows and
    rows of tall thin-leaved elms shaking
        in the window.
                      He didn't want to leap
  but leapt anyway, higher than
two hundred chandelier crystals, then fell
    like rain among us, the inviolable
clear-eyed people who never wanted
        to go this far:
                  past each bewildering
    field, the desiccating leaf piles, the little
blurred symbols for falling or turning
    back, until the strain of certain muscles
    propels us, like wind or feathers,
and Nijinsky, executing a fine
    tour jeté mid-air mid-anything,
    becomes, for a moment, possible . . .

As if we were dreams rooted dream-like
    to these locations, practically transparent
      and so so light—how we could fly then!

The

Here's a word for you!
The. The tree the chair
the wrinkles on the mother's
face the dreamings of the
child. The

is peculiar, not
designative, not evocative, an
introduction of sorts to the
objects of the perceptible
world—the man carrying the
canoe oars—and the invisible
one: the spirit the thought the
act of the imagination. The

is essentially inviolable, you
can't say good or bad the or what
an extraordinary the whose
"outside looks so fair and warlike."
You can't pick the out of the garden or
wrap the around your shoulders on a
cold night or take a walk with the

nor can the be bought or sold
or directed or timed or split apart
like they do to the tiniest of
particles with the tiniest of
hatchets. The

almighty and infinite the!
Consider the

ordinary person sitting on the
ordinary lawn chair. He thinks, if only
I could have the, life would be perfect,
they could take everything away from me
except the

The Black Puppy Story

Here comes the black puppy
with his ears and his snappy tail
and his wet eyes. You say
here comes the black puppy wanting
to come in or to be run over or
for his daily ration of beatings,
kicks to the ribs, a smack in the nose
and he whines, thank you, thank you.

The black puppy, we all think, is going
and then he's coming quick off the pink
porch, over the asphalt, speedy as a rocket.

You want to believe he's smiling
or that he's got a story of a lizard
who snatched at the brick wall
an armful of queen's wreath or a humble
slow-moving bug who gulps down the world
for power or dreams of power.

He smiles as he tells us.
Nothing is extraordinary. We whip him.
His wet dreamy eyes like the rest of us.

Not Nearly Enough

sun for the shoulders, breezes
for the head, not nearly enough
people here or true love drifting
in the afternoon here in Burlington,
I must be thinking of flies or do
I mean health, not nearly enough of
that in this body anyway, sleep all day,
listen to the volleyball game
through the window, music through
the flue, but not nearly enough deep
soul-touching jazzy magnets to pull
me out of this room that, come to think
of it, has not nearly enough light or
warmth for me to want to stay much longer.
all I do all day is sit in front of
a window that went black before I
woke up, during the dream (perhaps) I
had of you & me sitting somewhere, some
state or municipal building, a strange
impersonal green part of a bench between
us, but not nearly enough information
to reconstruct it.

Child Coloring a Ballerina

Unbravely chooses pink for pas de deux,
yellow for the sun. So much
she thinks is mystery and color covers up
ideas of it. Her hand adores the space
but strokes and sorrow-strokes are coming out
uncarefully. Children lose a way
to childhood where the background merely stops
half-way to masterpiece, when dancing on
and on becomes unbearable. Construct
it anyway, as if it somehow caught
the ballerina's dress; forget the air,
the buildings: earth and sky are thus undone
and almost to the point where they appear
again, unbrokenly undone and clear.

What's Missing

Through the black orange leaves
the lunar eclipse will be visible

like when we were never born
and the penumbras of our bodies

were extinguished, and the center
of, for example, childhood—

swinging from branches
or racing home—

was no longer history, but a circle
under a jar, where the light fails.

For these hours the air is like fire
and the small fire in our hearts

is like air or water, where a simple
dream of a canoe moving insistently

among white clouds
will shimmer with the undoing

of certain mysteries. And love
which can never occur

will float endlessly, brokenly beneath.

Poem Ending with a Sentence by Colette

Almost no one thinks we are immortal
and yet, proof to the contrary, we believe ourselves endlessly
flying off this way,
about to begin
without a moment's pause.
Here is the fingernail moon
we will climb and banter with, and so are stars.
Though faint
explosions can be heard spraying across Orion and the Pleiades,
the warm
almost enchanted wind envelops us.
In this way, sleep comes, just when you want it to. A gesture
tuned to the future, like a siren.
Did you ever think of it?
And did you ever think of that time called The Disarray of
    Dreams
when we want to bury beneath a few artifacts—
a scrap
of eucalyptus so like a stocking or a flower chosen from the
    many—
something even more personal.
It's like the letter I'll receive tomorrow—quite
possibly empty—except for the salutation, 'dear,'
which is perfect.
Or, when as a child, they said
whatever they said and we jittered to attention—
"Sleep between me and the fire,
to the purring of the cat
and the faint
rustling of the pages of the book I'm going to read now."

THREE

Heart-shaped Leaves

Begin with the sheen on your grandmother's
long bright scissors and the lilacs she cut.
And there is your grandfather on a lawn chair
under the mild wafting oak.

At such times
trailing your hand through a wave of light
or rolling a new beach ball into flowers
repeat what is sorrowful and familiar

as one day, we believe, rolls toward another
a precise history of disappearances
and always, in retrospect, there are details.

Like the heart-shaped leaves of lilac
crushed to her dress, and the careless
half-opened shape of scissors in the grass.
And although you never knew what agitated
the gaze of your grandfather, you can say
there was agitation and that, as he lifted
his old hand, as if to measure it,
there was a sharpness.

My Mother and the Shepherdess

The lamp is a woman
who is a shepherdess
who coyly gazes at my
mother who is sewing
with a white thread
the white hem of a dress.

The tiny veil is ringed
with lily-of-the-valley.
On the table
a prayer book, a silver
rosary, white cotton
gloves.
          She pulls the
needle through and it's
as if the dress itself
were breathing,

the stitches bringing
the dress to life
or the mother
or the girl whose
dress is breathing or

whose dress will bring
life to the girl who
holds her breath.
                    Who
looking at the shepherdess
feels the affinity
one feels with the merely
beautiful:

Under a tree
which is the lamp-post
and a sun which is only a lightbulb,
the little sheep by her shoes
sleep on
like nothing in this world
and nothing out of it.

Fiction

This poem wants to communicate
something of the look of my mother
who, when she folds her napkin precisely
at the same hour each evening, clinks
her fork onto her plate, is nevertheless
dreaming of times spent near the ocean.
Oh the boys and the beach balls and
the electric hour of youth when she seems
so remarkable and promising!
On the other hand, I can't ignore
my father who, when he dreams
dreams of the tallest building in Manhattan
and of himself teetering like a flower
and so vulnerable is the world, Daddy, that
growing like a weed, I revise them
until even their color of eyes
is uncertain and if the light crosses
at this or that instant who can anymore know?
My father hurls his napkin after meals
because anger is a virtue among men
and the constrained world of women
has made him unhappy. This is why
years ago he knocked some sense into my head:
Two bruises as beautiful as iris, and then
I flowered for him.

Eve II

When you say *Lover, look into my eyes*
I do, I do.
I see my miniature face rise

shape of obedience, size
of certain memories, point of view—
when you say *Lover, look into my eyes*

I never recognize
the you behind the you you want me to:
I see my miniature face rise

reflection that survives
itself, longing to see you through and through.
When you say *Lover, look into my eyes*

this is all I see—this prize
of diminution (*entre nous*),
I see my miniature face rise

continually, as lover after lover denies
herself. What more can I give you?
When you say *Lover, look into my eyes*
I see my miniature face arise.

Florida

On North Ocean Boulevard the stars
drifted in a loose geographical
parade each night as we adolescent
girls paraded for the cruising black
Thunderbirds, the fiery 'Vettes of 1960.
Paraded our shoulders, our slipping-around
halter tops, we'd try to wave them down
with smiles or sheer bold eye contact
out in front of the curling monumental
waves, the flat Florida sky—
Leaning against the lifeguard station,
ponytails sweeping the wind,
we tasted salt on our mouths and on
the boys' mouths under the stars'
random beam and the accidental way
we did anything then—
And we'd be transfigured in the moonlight,
almost other-worldly, waiting
for the boys to come, for the screech
of wheels on asphalt, for the casual
lowering of headlights which meant that any
minute we'd be walking away with them
down the hard beach toward the abandoned
cabanas—
In 1960, those feelings welled around us
in the dark hot air as we waited—
I like to remember our shining ethereal
faces and the way we thought love
could transform us, and the way,
in those times of waiting, the stars
flickered beautifully overhead
and we were not aware of their configuration
and we were not aware of our own.

Resurrecting My Sister

In the pale frozen light
of thirty years ago
my sister and I wear matching
coats, straw hats, carry
new red purses, cotton
gloves. We are someone's

definition of Easter Sunday—
eyes pinned to the viewfinder,
stunned out of fidgeting,
trees behind us.

Back and to the left
a spire, then a cross against
clouds, and in front six purple
crocuses, a handkerchief,
part of a shadow.

In the photograph
I am the older one, the one
with the bent hat-brim, the raw
patch of skin creeping above the sock;
Look! I am crushing my sister's tiny hand
in mine! See how I stoop! See how I
wince in the sun! See my little ugly
face, my terrible uncombed hair!

You wanted to know about my sister
et voilà! she returns, goes straight
to the empty slot beside me:
knuckles under knuckles under
perfect, shiny and surviving.

Another New Movie

On the page I come across
more heavenly than flesh, as it should be:
Here the flimsy character weeps
or leans, we have to reinvent each time
we lose her. Think of those modern advertisements
bleeding across the hills, the strange
wide bones of an image. Little
facets of memory—glass-topped, oak and wafting,
the textures jingling on your throat.
Girls in matching outfits,
hair pulled into ribbons, we are
simple and complete, the two of us—I say the sky
looks pale and memorable, drinking Scotch, Sunday,
swinging, the yellow curvy moment
of birth, black and white versions of time
reeling along.

Winter

At this distance our mother is so simplified.
She is in her apron while the toast pops, singing
to the old radio *kiss me once and kiss me*
twice and we kiss her and we eat. You should
have heard her laugh, should have seen her hair,
chestnut brown, and her brownest eyes. She rinsed her hands

under the tap, then taught us how to use our hands,
cracking an egg into a bowl, a simplified
gesture of life, she said; she kept our long hair
back from our faces so we could watch the yellow singing
of the yolk change like a miracle, as it should
change, she taught us. She used to say *children trust me*

but there was no other we could trust, which made me
cautious and less vulnerable. She almost hands
us everything—the whole world on our plates—but should
we believe her, she seems to ask. From this simplified
distance we can believe the beautiful aproned woman singing
kiss me or trust me. She feeds us, gathers our hair

in top-knots before bed, closes the blinds. Her hair
meanwhile brushes our faces very softly; makes me
want to sleep, but I listen instead to the singing
of the two children in *The Snow Queen* by Hans
Christian Andersen. They are singing a simplified
version of a prayer, something about roses and should

the Christ Child appear, how he would preserve them; should
roses bloom or decay, it wouldn't matter. My mother's hair
moves across the story which is the simplified
story of our lives with her. The Snow Queen says *trust me*
to the children and the children accept her hands
which are like icicles, mount her sturdy sled singing

the only words they knew about. We keep on singing
them because there were never others, if we should
stop and look around, no one whose beautiful hair
conducts our wandering glances to hands
that teach us how to become ourselves. Now I say *trust me*
to my daughters, I carry them off to simplified

winters where we sing what women should be singing,
what is small and eternal, the way our hands and hair
simplify this cold wind blowing distantly through me.

Hunter/Hunted

The children bring a half-dead baby
bird into the house. Pink with
four feathers, smaller than a
walnut.

                He is lying
on a bed of ripped-up leaves
inside a paper cup torn open
at the rim.

             Through his beak
(golden blue-veined transparency)
emerges the pale end of a worm
the children have stuffed down.

              His haunches
curl at the hip like human
fetus haunches and one wing
thick as a grass blade, bends
upwards in the wrong position.

With an eyedropper
                    we squeeze beads
of water down his throat; the pink
body shudders, the human
children take heart, eyes
bright as berries, soft soft
mouths.

Grandfather

What can I say to you, in your fat grave
your body no longer inside itself?
Here is a mound, remarkable
form of a wave, which
in its momentary lapses
is simply gathering what has been lost
and repeating it.
Here, then, you are.
Your skin, closer to angels, your
large generous hands resting, as was their custom,
and the interlocking gold ring
from which memory will finally engrave
itself with your initials is present
and absent at the same time.
We are growing apart
as distance is beleaguered by silence
whiter than carnations; and closer
as the mind adjusts to your memory:
As we cannot do.
For there you were, sitting on the green
bench, eyes even then wandering beyond
as if toward some future and arresting
landscape. And we, the objects of the real world,
colorfully arranged, as we are bound to be.

Irresistibly, the Heart Opens

Irresistibly, the heart opens, just as once in the summer
those boys slid right down the mud rock
and we wondered where they came from and if, handsome
and abstracted as they seemed, they thought we were pretty.
The heavy foliage reeking of jungle movies, the long
swing out over, the smell of mud or the safe hot feel of it
between our toes . . . we watched those boys swing mindlessly
out over, or slide down mud rock, their faces pressed
to the air, their hands rough as trees. And we were pretty
then, we were beautiful in our odd ways, our wet hair, our
narrow shoulders and little hard grasping fingers
of girls. The boys slid down, how their dark eyes
turned us on, those dark boy eyes aroused us
in their handsome abstraction, caring for nothing but
the particular moment of sliding, the touch
of muscle to water, the wild heaving of space—

The Wondrousness of Light and Other Problems

It is never a question of the
wondrousness of light, no more
than legs or trees or the fact
that in the winter water freezes
outside and bodies who would otherwise
be gazing into a dangerous and reflected
mystery, skate along.

          It happens I have a view
of them through this window, so seamlessly
immediate it makes me think I'm dreaming.
Last night my daughter explained her method
for inventing stories, *just pretend
it's a dream you're having, imagine you're
having a dream.* Like the swans out there
have somehow prevented one place in the lake
from freezing up so they can continue to paddle
right through my sense of them, all winter.

It seems that, if anything, light is a metaphor
for what happens to the life of anyone, the way
it moves, always slowly, across a given area
now exposing, now failing so that the whole scheme
becomes less defined. On the other hand,
a scene may exist beneath anything—a log
or a house—or the universe of bugs and moles,
like the imaginings of my daughter who,
when she thought of a dream thought
of what Superman would say when he saw her
on the swing set, trying to get higher.
He'd say *let go, just let go.*

Meanwhile the best we seem to be able to achieve
is in photographs of light, light traveling up
the knee or shoulder of some loved one.
And is it truth or union with truth that we
are after, annihilation or power? So many
important questions while in the next room
the children talk about sleighriding, the snow
is pretty good packing snow. And for me
there is amazement in being able to see
the sun shining on the edge of the lake so bright
it is like gold, and on the edge of a roof covered
with snow and the edge of a book of notes by Claes
Oldenburg that I propped on the sill two months ago.

I am also taken aback to find that the older
I get the less true anything seems. Was it
Ponge with a kind of French disdain who confessed
he was no good at ideas and actually not very
intelligent, but that he believed in details
that it was important to be able to describe
the difference between a walnut and a praline?
                        And now, because the light
has crossed the lake just enough so it looks almost
transparent, even from here, I imagine Scylla
underneath, so beautifully detailed that Glaucus,
the monster, loved her. Eventually, paralyzed
in the ocean, a detail of paradox,
she is swaying in her long tentacles, unable
to go anywhere.

And the light is so impersonal, the lack of idea it has
about it. Look how it seems to grow larger in the sky
how the trees seem to burn!
                              On the other side of the lake
a row of cottages, and the moon's watery rise.
Already the skaters are leaving,
leaving the most delicate etchings on a surface
composed of the most delicate molecular responses.

About the Author

Karen Brennan wrote puppet shows, plays, stories, and poems as a child. Now an author of fiction and plays as well as of poetry, she received an Academy of American Poets Prize at the University of Arizona in 1986, the Sonora Review Poetry Prize the same year, and a P.E.N. Syndicated Short Fiction Award in 1987.

Brennan was born in New Rochelle, New York, and grew up in Larchmont. She earned a B.A. at Newton College of the Sacred Heart, in Newton, Massachusetts (1963), and an M.F.A. at Goddard College (1979). She is now studying for her Ph.D. and teaches at the University of Arizona. She has four children and her home is in Tucson.

About the Book

Here on Earth was composed on a Compugraphic MCS 100 Digital Typesetting System in Goudy Old Style, a typeface designed by Frederic W. Goudy. Frederic Goudy, a Midwestern accountant turned letterer and type designer, set up the Village Press at Park Ridge, Illinois, and became probably the most prolific type designer in printing history.

The book was composed by Lithocraft Company of Grundy Center, Iowa, and designed by Kachergis Book Design, Pittsboro, North Carolina.

WESLEYAN UNIVERSITY PRESS, 1988